WHAT DO YOU KNOW ABOUT

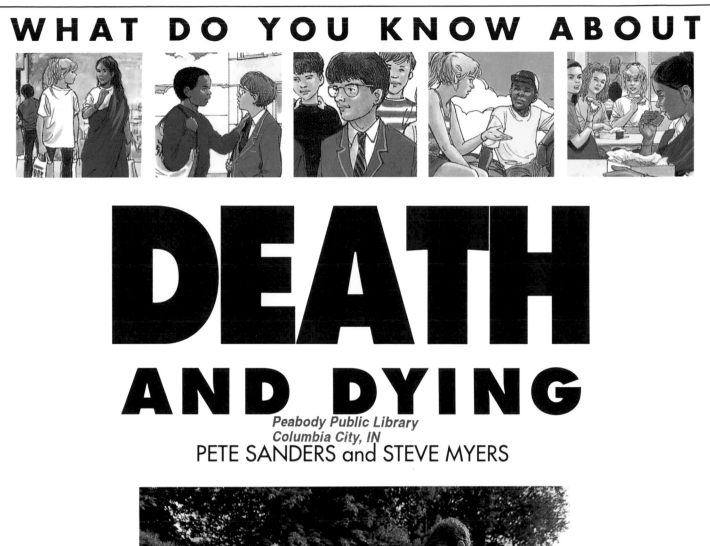

DEATH
AND DYING

Peabody Public Library
Columbia City, IN

PETE SANDERS and STEVE MYERS

COPPER BEECH BOOKS

BROOKFIELD, CONNECTICUT

Designed and produced by
Aladdin Books Ltd
28 Percy Street
London W1P 0LD

First published
in the United States in 1998 by
Copper Beech Books,
an imprint of
The Millbrook Press
2 Old New Milford Road
Brookfield, Connecticut 06804

Printed in Belgium

Design   David West
                Children's Book
                Design
Editor   Sarah Levete
Picture research Brooks Krikler
                Research
Illustrator   Mike Lacey

Library of Congress
Cataloging-in-Publication Data
Sanders, Pete.
Death and dying / Pete Sanders and Steve
Myers ; illustrated by Mike Lacey.
p. cm. — (What do you know about)
Includes index.
Summary: Explores the feelings and issues that
may arise after the death of a loved one and the
importance of confronting such issues.
ISBN 0-7613-0872-5 (lib. bdg.)
1. Children and death—Juvenile literature.
2. Death—Psychological aspects—Juvenile
literature. 3. Bereavement in children—Juvenile
literature. 4. Bereavement—Psychological
aspects. 5. Grief in children—Juvenile literature.
6. Grief—Juvenile literature.
[1. Death. 2. Grief.] I. Myers, Steve. II. Lacey,
Mike, ill. III. Title. IV. Series: Sanders, Pete.
What do you know about.
BF713.D3S26 1998   98-16968
155.9'37—dc21   CIP AC

CONTENTS

HOW TO USE THIS BOOK

The books in this series are intended to help young people to understand more about issues that may affect their lives.

Each book can be read by a child alone, or together with a parent, teacher, or guardian. Issues raised in the storyline are further discussed in the accompanying text, so that there is an opportunity to talk through ideas as they come up.

At the end of the book there is a section called "What Can We Do?" This gives practical ideas that will be useful for both young people and adults. Organizations and helplines are also listed, to provide the reader with additional sources of information and support.

INTRODUCTION

DEATH AND DYING ARE A NATURAL PART OF THE CYCLE OF LIFE.

However, many people find the subject of death and dying very hard to talk about, because it means confronting issues and emotions that they find difficult to deal with.

This book explains what death and dying mean. It looks at some of the feelings and issues that might be raised and the kinds of reaction people may show at the death of someone close. Each chapter introduces a different aspect of the subject, illustrated by a continuing storyline. The characters in the story deal with situations and feelings that many people will experience. After each episode, we stop and look at some of the issues raised, and broaden the discussion. By the end, you will understand more about death and dying and how they can affect everyone involved.

> IT'S NOT LIKE THAT ANNIE. WHEN PATCH DIED, YOU WERE VERY YOUNG AND WE DIDN'T EXPLAIN IT TO YOU VERY WELL.

> DEATH ISN'T LIKE GOING TO SLEEP, DARLING. SLEEP HELPS YOUR BODY TO REST, SO THAT IT CAN WORK PROPERLY. EVERYBODY NEEDS SLEEP.

DEATH

DEATH IS SOMETHING WE WILL ALL HAVE TO FACE AT SOME POINT. IT IS NOT SOMETHING TO BE FEARED.

Death is when the body stops working. This usually means that the heart stops beating, the brain no longer functions, and a person stops breathing.

There are many different reasons for this happening. Most of us, especially when we are young, expect to follow the natural process of life and live to an old age. For a great many people, death comes as a result of the natural effects of age on the body. However, death can be caused by other factors, and does not just happen to elderly people. Accidents, or even the deliberate actions of another person, can

cause death. Some people have taken their own lives because of great unhappiness. Someone's state of health throughout life can affect their likelihood of developing a condition that might prove fatal. This is why doctors and other people stress the need to look after yourself at all stages of your life by eating a healthy, balanced diet and getting plenty of exercise. Medical advances mean that many diseases that at one time would have resulted in a person's death can now be cured. However, certain illnesses remain incurable. These are sometimes called terminal illnesses.

Today, better social conditions and a greater awareness of health issues mean that we tend to live to an older age.

▽ One day, Tina Burton and her brother, Mark, met up with some friends after school to play.

WHAT'S WRONG, DOMINIC? AREN'T YOU COMING IN?

I DON'T LIKE PLAYING IN THERE. IT'S CREEPY.

IT'S PERFECT FOR PLAYING SPACE WARS. COME ON, DON'T BE A COWARD.

▽ Reluctantly, Dominic joined them. Soon, they were all pretending to have a battle.

MISSED ME!

NO I DIDN'T, SUNIL. I SHOT YOU. YOU'RE DEAD.

▽ A short while later, Dominic realized he couldn't see his friends anymore. They were all hiding from him.

WWHHHHHOOOO!

COME ON, YOU GUYS. THIS ISN'T FUNNY.

▽ Carol suddenly leapt out from behind one of the gravestones, making Dominic jump.

YOU IDIOT! YOU SCARED ME. ANYHOW, WE SHOULDN'T BE PLAYING HERE. IT ISN'T RIGHT.

WE'RE NOT DOING ANY HARM.

DAVE'S RIGHT. COME ON, LET'S PLAY.

▽ Mark ran off, chased by Tina and Sunil.

I GOT YOU, MARK!

AAAARRRGH!

WHAT DO YOU THINK YOU ARE DOING? THIS ISN'T A PLAYGROUND. YOU, GET UP. THAT'S MY SON'S GRAVE. DON'T YOU HAVE ANY RESPECT?

△ They all apologized and began to walk away. Mark felt really bad about what had happened.

▽ He told the others to wait, and turned back to the woman.

I DIDN'T MEAN TO UPSET YOU. I WASN'T THINKING. MOM'S ALWAYS TELLING ME ABOUT THAT. I'M REALLY SORRY.

THAT'S OK. MY FRANKIE WAS JUST THE SAME. HE WOULD HAVE BEEN ABOUT YOUR AGE NOW.

▽ The woman told Mark her name was Mrs. Idika. Her son had been killed in a car crash a year earlier.

MY GRANDPA IS BURIED OVER THERE. I DON'T UNDERSTAND WHY PEOPLE HAVE TO DIE. IT SEEMS SO UNFAIR.

I KNOW. THE HOSPITAL DID EVERYTHING THEY COULD FOR FRANKIE, BUT IN THE END THEY COULDN'T SAVE HIM.

▽ Mark told Mrs. Idika that his grandmother was very ill now.

SHE'S LIVED WITH US SINCE GRANDPA DIED, BUT SHE'S BEEN IN THE HOSPITAL SOME OF THE TIME. I DON'T REALLY KNOW WHAT'S WRONG WITH HER, BUT I THINK IT'S WORSE THAN MOM AND DAD ARE SAYING.

MARK, ARE YOU COMING? WE SHOULD BE GETTING BACK.

▽ Mark said goodbye to Mrs. Idika and left with Tina.

YOU SHOULDN'T HAVE BEEN TALKING ABOUT GRANDMA LIKE THAT. YOU DIDN'T KNOW THAT WOMAN. YOU KNOW THAT MOM AND DAD HAVE TOLD US NOT TO TALK TO STRANGERS.

I KNOW, BUT YOU AND THE OTHERS WERE THERE. I WANTED TO APOLOGIZE.

DON'T BE SO MORBID. I'M SURE MOM AND DAD WOULD HAVE TOLD US IF THERE WAS ANYTHING SERIOUSLY WRONG.

I'M NOT SO CERTAIN. THEY'VE BEEN REALLY SECRETIVE LATELY.

MRS. IDIKA SEEMED NICE. SHE WAS TELLING ME ABOUT HER SON DYING. IT MADE ME THINK ABOUT GRANDMA. MAYBE SHE'S DYING. I THINK SHE'S REALLY ILL.

△ As they made their way home, Tina began to wonder if Mark might be right.

Like Mark and his friends, lots of young people enjoy playing games. Often these are based on events from T.V. shows or movies, and involve pretend violence where characters use imaginary weapons to "kill" each other. Some adults worry about the effect these games can have on those who play them. They believe that they encourage young people to see violence as acceptable.

It is important to separate the fiction of the game from the facts of real life. Because we see so much "pretend" death on T.V., it can be tempting to think of death as something very remote.

In movies, characters often survive incidents that nobody could survive in reality. Some young people have been seriously injured trying to copy the kind of actions they have seen their favorite actors doing.

Tina is worried that her mom and dad may not be telling her the truth about Grandma. Adults often find it difficult to talk about death and dying, particularly to children. They may believe they are sparing young people unnecessary worry and pain. But not talking about a situation might cause much anxiety and may make it more difficult to deal with.

The friends did not intend to upset Mrs. Idika. However, Mrs. Idika thought that it was insensitive of them to play such a game in a cemetery, and that it showed a lack of respect for her dead son and the others buried there. When people die, they are no longer a part of the physical world around us. However, the memory of the dead person can be very important to friends and family. It can be distressing if others do not seem to respect it.

DYING

DEATH IS THE MOMENT AT WHICH LIFE ENDS. IT CAN ALSO MEAN THE EVENT OR PROCESS THAT RESULTS IN A PERSON'S DEATH.

This might happen very quickly or it may take a long time.
People will sometimes say that they are not frightened of death itself, but that they are afraid of dying. They may see some ways of dying as "worse" than others, perhaps because they involve some suffering for the dying person. The way in which a person dies might affect the reaction of other people to his or her death. Some people are told that they are going to die – perhaps because they have an illness that cannot be cured. When this happens, the effect on them and those close to them can be devastating. Everyone will react differently. Certain emotions, however, are common to many people. At first, there may be disbelief at the news, as people try to deny the truth of what they have been told. They may become angry, asking why this should be happening to them or to someone they love. Most will experience periods of great sadness. It is not unusual to experience these emotions.

Just because someone knows that he or she is dying, this does not necessarily prevent him or her from enjoying life.

▽ Two days later, Tina and Mark's younger sister, Annie, was helping Mrs. Burton to prepare a meal.

WHAT'S THE MATTER WITH YOU TWO? YOU LOOK VERY SERIOUS.

WE WANT TO ASK YOU SOMETHING.

WE WANT TO KNOW WHAT'S REALLY WRONG WITH GRANDMA. SHE'S MUCH WORSE THAN SHE USED TO BE.

▽ Mrs. Burton was surprised. She sat down at the table.

IS SHE GOING TO DIE?

ANNIE, WHY DON'T YOU GO AND PUT YOUR NEW VIDEO ON DARLING? I WANT TO SPEAK TO MARK AND TINA FOR A MOMENT.

▽ Annie happily ran into the other room. Mrs. Burton said she would speak to her later. Mark could tell she was close to tears.

YOU KNOW EVERYONE HAS TO DIE AT SOME TIME. YOUR GRANDMA HAS A SERIOUS ILLNESS. SHE'S HAD A LOT OF TREATMENT, BUT THE DOCTORS CAN'T DO ANY MORE FOR HER. SHE'S DYING.

▽ Mark and Tina were both very upset.

HOW LONG WILL SHE LIVE?

NOBODY KNOWS, DARLING. BUT SHE'S GOING TO NEED A LOT OF CARE AND ATTENTION.

WE'LL LOOK AFTER HER.

IT'S NOT AS EASY AS THAT, I'M AFRAID. YOUR GRANDMA WILL NEED MORE SPECIALIZED CARE AND HELP THAN WE CAN GIVE HER AT HOME. YOUR DAD AND I HAVE BEEN TALKING ABOUT TRYING TO FIND HER A PLACE IN A HOSPICE.

THEY'LL HAVE THE STAFF AND FACILITIES TO CARE REALLY WELL FOR YOUR GRANDMA. YOU'LL STILL BE ABLE TO VISIT HER WHENEVER YOU WANT.

△ Mark and Tina both asked what a hospice was. Mrs. Burton explained.

▽ Later on, Annie asked her parents what it meant to die. She had overheard Mark and Tina talking.

WHEN MY DOG, PATCH, GOT SICK YOU TOLD ME HE WAS GOING TO SLEEP FOR A LONG TIME AND I WOULDN'T BE ABLE TO SEE HIM ANYMORE. IS THAT WHAT'S GOING TO HAPPEN TO GRANDMA? THAT'S SCARY. WHAT IF I GO TO SLEEP AND NEVER WAKE UP? WHAT IF I DIE LIKE GRANDMA'S GOING TO?

IT'S NOT LIKE THAT ANNIE. WHEN PATCH DIED, YOU WERE VERY YOUNG AND WE DIDN'T EXPLAIN IT TO YOU VERY WELL.

DEATH ISN'T LIKE GOING TO SLEEP, DARLING. SLEEP HELPS YOUR BODY TO REST SO THAT IT CAN WORK PROPERLY. EVERYBODY NEEDS SLEEP.

WHEN PEOPLE DIE IT MEANS THAT THE BODY STOPS WORKING COMPLETELY. ALTHOUGH WE DON'T SEE THEM ANYMORE, PEOPLE LIVE IN OUR MEMORIES, JUST AS YOU'RE REMEMBERING PATCH.

◁ Annie asked a few more questions. Her mom and dad tried to answer them as honestly as possible.

▽ The next morning, Mark was preparing breakfast for Grandma.

DO YOU WANT TO TAKE GRANDMA'S TRAY INTO HER? SHE SAYS SHE HASN'T SEEN YOU LATELY.

I DON'T THINK I CAN GO INTO HER ROOM. I DON'T WANT TO SEE HER. IT MAKES ME FEEL REALLY UNCOMFORTABLE.

I FELT A BIT LIKE THAT AT FIRST. AFTER WE FOUND OUT, IT WAS ODD—I DIDN'T KNOW WHETHER TO TALK ABOUT IT. BUT WHEN I SAW HER I REALIZED THAT'S SHE'S STILL GRANDMA. YOU'LL FEEL WORSE IF YOU DON'T SEE HER.

I'VE BROUGHT YOU YOUR BREAKFAST GRANDMA.

THAT'S KIND OF YOU, DEAR. TINA, IT'S LOVELY TO SEE YOU. WHY DON'T YOU COME IN AND SIT ON THE BED AND TALK TO ME FOR A WHILE?

△ Eventually, Tina did spend some time with Grandma. She was pleased she had overcome her worries.

Tina is unsure how to treat Grandma.
Some people's own fears about death can influence their behavior. This may cause awkwardness in their relationship with the other person. It is natural to experience some uncertainty. For instance, you might be afraid of upsetting the person and believe that you should not cry or show any emotion. But it is likely that someone who is dying will want you to treat him or her in just the same way as you always have done.

Grandma will need a lot of care and attention.
Some people can be cared for at home. Others may need hospital treatment. People who are dying may be able to stay in a hospice for a short while before going back home or until their death. Whatever the situation, someone who is dying deserves to be treated with dignity.

Finding the right words to describe death and dying can be difficult.
It is very hard for some adults, who are unsure how to discuss the issues with young people. This can mean that information is unclear. Like Annie, many younger children might easily misunderstand messages like "he's gone to sleep" or "she's gone away for a very long time." This can be very confusing and frightening. Clear discussion of the subject can help to avoid any unnecessary fears and worries.

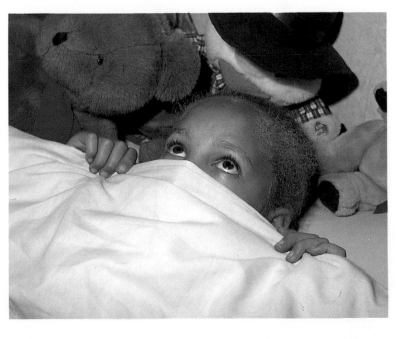

HOW DO PEOPLE FEEL ABOUT DEATH AND DYING?

PEOPLE'S ATTITUDES TOWARD DEATH AND DYING CAN VARY A GREAT DEAL.

Because life is very precious to most of us, our feelings about death are sometimes surrounded by uncertainty and fear.

Many people are reluctant to talk about the subject. They may fear that doing so somehow brings death nearer. Some see death as affecting only elderly people, so they think that it need not concern them. But facing up to the subject can help us to cope with our feelings and those of others around us, when we become directly affected by the death of someone close. Discussion of death and dying means confronting particular concerns, such as anxiety about what happens after death, worry about what will happen to those you love, and a fear of being separated from them. People might also be afraid that dying involves physical pain, or that they will need someone else to look after them if they are very ill.

However, many people are able to accept that dying is a natural part of life and not something to be feared. But this does not always mean that if someone close to them dies, their feelings will be less strong or easier to deal with.

Some people enjoy the risks and excitement of taking part in "death-defying" sports or pursuits.

▽ A few weeks later, in the playground, Mark and his friends were talking about a new boy who had arrived at school.

THAT'S JOSEF. HE'S A REFUGEE. HE'S JUST STARTED IN MY CLASS. I HEARD THAT BOTH HIS PARENTS HAD BEEN KILLED. HE'S LIVING WITH FOSTER PARENTS IN THIS COUNTRY NOW.

IT MUST BE AWFUL. I'VE SEEN PHOTOGRAPHS OF THE FIGHTING ON THE NEWS, BUT IT ALL SEEMS SO FAR AWAY.

I CAN'T THINK HOW I'D FEEL IF THAT HAPPENED TO MY FAMILY.

▽ In another part of the playground, Carol and Tina were talking about Tina's grandma.

THE PEOPLE AT THE HOSPICE ARE GOOD, BUT I CAN'T STAND TO SEE GRANDMA IN SO MUCH PAIN.

I DON'T THINK I COULD GO THROUGH WITH IT. I'D RATHER DIE QUICKLY THAN SUFFER—I'D EVEN ASK THE DOCTORS TO GIVE ME SOMETHING TO DO IT.

AT'S A TERRIBLE THING TO Y. LIFE'S ALWAYS GOT TO BETTER THAN DEATH, NO TTER WHAT THE CIRCUM- ANCES ARE. WHAT IF THE CTORS WERE ABLE TO D A CURE TOMORROW?

◁ The boys were passing and overheard Tina and Carol talking.

I READ THAT IN SOME COUNTRIES IT'S LEGAL FOR DOCTORS TO HELP PEOPLE DIE, IF THERE'S NO HOPE OF THEM GETTING BETTER AND THE PERSON WANTS IT TO HAPPEN.

IT DEPENDS ON YOUR RELIGION, TOO. I DON'T BELIEVE ANYONE HAS THE RIGHT TO TAKE A LIFE.

△ Everybody began to talk about how they felt.

DO YOU HAVE TO TALK ABOUT DEATH SO MUCH? I DON'T LIKE IT. IT'S LIKE TEMPTING FATE, OR SOMETHING.

DON'T BE SILLY! YOU'RE JUST SUPERSTITIOUS.

COME ON. LET'S GO OVER AND SEE IF JOSEF WANTS TO PLAY WITH US.

WHAT ARE YOU DOING, MOM? ARE THOSE GRANDMA'S?

YES. YOUR GRANDMA ASKED ME TO GO OVER EVERYTHING TO MAKE SURE IT'S ALL IN ORDER. SHE MADE A WILL, BUT IT'S BEEN A WHILE SINCE SHE LOOKED AT IT. SOME THINGS MIGHT NEED TO BE UPDATED.

△ The group went over to Josef.

▷ When he arrived home that evening, Mark found his mom going through some papers.

13

Mrs. Burton is making certain that her mother's will is in order.
A will is a legal document that gives details of your instructions – for example, that you want money or property to go to a particular person. Making preparations for what will happen to you and your belongings after your death enables other people to respect your wishes. This can help to avoid problems and misunderstandings. Many people choose to carry donor cards so that doctors will be able to use their organs after their death to help others who need a transplant.

Josef's parents have been killed in a war.
The death of a parent or guardian can be bewildering for young people because it may mean practical changes in who looks after them. At an early age, Josef has had to come to terms with the death of his family.

This has not been caused by illness or old age, but by war. It can be especially difficult to understand and accept the death of someone close when it has been caused by the action of another person, either deliberately or accidentally.

Carol thinks that she would prefer to be helped to die rather than to live in pain.
Causing the death of someone, with his or her consent, to avoid further suffering is called euthanasia. It is illegal in most countries, though in some it is legal under very special circumstances. There is much debate about this subject. Many people believe that, no matter what, nobody has the right to end a life or take any action that would lead to another person's death. Others believe that each person should have the right to choose, depending on his or her own situation.

WHAT HAPPENS AFTER YOU DIE?

THERE ARE MANY DIFFERENT IDEAS ABOUT WHAT HAPPENS TO US AFTER WE DIE, BUT THERE IS NO RIGHT OR WRONG ANSWER.

Some people have very strong views that are often based on their religion or culture.

According to some people, we are all made up of two parts – the physical body and an invisible element, sometimes called the spirit or soul. It is this that they think is the most important part of our being, which makes us what we are and which gives us our personality. They believe that, although the body decays after death, the soul or immortal spirit of the person is "released" and continues to exist in some way. Many people talk about heaven and hell – places to which the soul is sent, depending on whether a person was "good" or "bad" while alive. Some people and religions talk about reincarnation, believing that the soul is reborn as another

person or creature. Others do not think anything happens to us when we die – that it is simply the end. You may have your own opinions about the subject. Many people feel very strongly about their beliefs. It is important to remember that everyone is entitled to his or her own view.

Some believe very strongly in an "after-life" – that the soul continues to exist although the body is no longer part of the physical world. It is very important for them to show respect to this world of souls and spirits.

▽ A few weeks later, Tina and Mark were visiting Grandma in the hospice. They began to talk about Grandpa.

I CAN REMEMBER WHEN WE USED TO STAY WITH YOU. GRANDPA USED TO TELL THESE FANTASTIC STORIES.

YEAH. MOSTLY THEY WERE SUPPOSED TO BE BEDTIME STORIES, BUT THEY WERE SO GOOD, WE WOULDN'T GO TO SLEEP.

GRANPA COULD ALWAYS TELL A GOOD STORY.

▽ That weekend, Tina and Mark decided to visit their grandpa's grave.

IT'S HORRIBLE TO THINK GRANDMA'S GOING TO BE BURIED HERE SOON.

I'M GOING TO MISS HER SO MUCH. WHAT DO YOU THINK HAPPENS TO YOU WHEN YOU DIE? DO YOU THINK GRANDMA AND GRANDPA WILL BE TOGETHER AGAIN SOMEWHERE?

I'D LIKE TO THINK SO. NOBODY REALLY KNOWS WHAT HAPPENS TO YOU, DO THEY? DO YOU THINK WE HAVE A SOUL-OR SOMETHING THAT LEAVES OUR BODY WHEN WE DIE?

I DON'T KNOW BUT I DON'T THINK DEATH CAN JUST BE THE END OF EVERYTHING. I USED TO THINK GRANDPA WAS SOMEWHERE WATCHING ME.

SO DID I. I THOUGHT HE WAS LOOKING OUT FOR ME. IT FELT GOOD, BUT ALSO A BIT ODD, AS THOUGH HE'D KNOW IF I EVER DID SOMETHING WRONG.

▽ The boy said he was Frankie's brother, Julian. They all started chatting.

△ Mark had noticed a boy standing by Frankie's grave. He went over to him.

I COME HERE EVERY WEEK, AND TALK TO FRANKIE. I DON'T LIKE TO STAY TOO LATE, THOUGH. I WOULDN'T WANT TO BE HERE WHEN IT'S DARK, IN CASE THERE ARE ANY GHOSTS.

I WAS ONLY TRYING TO SCARE YOU. IT WAS A SILLY THING TO SAY.

WE ARE GOING TO GET A BURGER. DO YOU WANT TO COME WITH US?

DON'T BE SILLY. THERE ARE NO SUCH THINGS AS GHOSTS. THAT'S JUST IN STORIES.

SOME PEOPLE BELIEVE IN THEM, THOUGH. THERE ARE ALL KINDS OF IDEAS ABOUT WHAT HAPPENS TO YOU WHEN YOU DIE.

△ Julian accepted. They all left to go into town.

Like Mark and Tina, many people feel as if the dead person still cares for and protects them.
This can feel very comforting. At times we might think that they can see everything we are doing. Sometimes adults will tell young people this in order to try to control their behavior. This is not a good idea and can be very frightening, especially for younger children.

Mark and Tina have enjoyed talking about Grandpa with Grandma.
Remembering someone who has died is very important to most people. It may be a memory of a special time spent together, a favorite photograph, a particular place, or even a smell, which calls to mind something about the person. Some people, however, find it difficult to be around things that remind them of the dead person.

Memories can make you feel both happy and sad. Sometimes people tend to concentrate only on the happy ones. This can lead to them idealizing the person who has died. But there is nothing wrong with remembering sad times or things you did not like about the person as well. Nor is there anything wrong in enjoying your life – you do not need to feel guilty for this.

Julian has tried to frighten the others by talking about ghosts.
You have probably read stories or watched movies about places that are supposed to be haunted by the spirits of dead people. Some people believe in ghosts; others do not. Unusual events are sometimes said to be caused by spirits. It may be that the strength of our imagination is responsible for some unexplained events. Nothing has been proved either way. Whatever the case, it is not something to be frightened of.

REACTIONS TO LOSS

LOSING SOMEBODY CLOSE, THROUGH DEATH, IS CALLED BEREAVEMENT.

People can have very different reactions to the loss of a loved one. It may depend on the individual and the relationship with the person who has died. The way that someone has died can also affect the way we react to the news, as can the age of both the deceased and the person being told about his or her death. Other factors may be the role of the dead person in people's lives, and what his or her death will mean in practical terms – if it means having to move, for example. Often the initial response is a feeling of shock. This may be more extreme if a death is sudden. But it can still be the case when a person had been ill for a long time and death had been expected at some point. Shock and numbness will usually then give way to grief.

Our feelings often take us by surprise. Some people might appear to show no immediate reaction but this does not necessarily mean that they do not care or feel deeply. Every person has an individual response to sad news.

The loss of someone close can cause many different and confusing emotions. Some of these may be influenced by the type and strength of the relationship you shared.

▽ A month later, Tina and Mark came down to breakfast to find their mom crying.

WHAT'S GOING ON? WHY'S MOM CRYING?

I'VE A HORRBLE FEELING I KNOW. I THOUGHT I HEARD THE PHONE RING IN THE MIDDLE OF THE NIGHT. IT'S GRANDMA, ISN'T IT?

I'M AFRAID SO.

SHE TOOK A TURN FOR THE WORSE LAST NIGHT. WE ASKED MRS. WHITE FROM NEXT DOOR TO STAY WITH YOU WHILE WE WENT TO THE HOSPICE. SHE DIED AN HOUR AFTER WE ARRIVED.

NO! GRANDMA CAN'T BE DEAD.

△ Mark began to cry. Mr. Burton sat them down and explained what had happened.

YOU SHOULD HAVE WOKEN US UP. WE COULD HAVE GONE WITH YOU.

I NEVER SAID GOODBYE OR TOLD HER HOW MUCH I LOVED HER. I SHOULD HAVE GONE TO VISIT HER MORE. NOW I'LL NEVER SEE HER AGAIN.

I'M SORRY DARLING. WE DID WHAT WE THOUGHT WAS THE BEST. YOUR GRANDMA DIED VERY PEACEFULLY.

IT'S STRANGE. EVEN THOUGH I KNEW GRANDMA WAS GOING TO DIE, IT STILL FEELS BAD.

I KNOW YOUR GRANDPA DIED SUDDENLY, AND THAT WAS AN AWFUL SHOCK. THIS IS DIFFERENT. BUT I THINK GETTING OVER IT IS GOING TO BE JUST AS DIFFICULT. I CAN'T BELIEVE SHE'S GONE.

I FEEL SO SAD, BUT I CAN'T CRY.

△ Tina and Mark realized how their mom must be feeling. After a while, everyone was able to talk more calmly.

△ Mr. Burton told Tina that not everybody cries when they are sad. He said it can take time for feelings to sink in.

▽ Annie had been standing just outside the door. She suddenly burst into tears and ran upstairs.

▽ The next day at school, Carol told Tina she was sorry to hear of her grandma's death.

ANNIE, DARLING. IT'S OK.

I'LL GO. I DIDN'T REALIZE SHE WAS LISTENING. SHE SHOULDN'T HAVE HEARD ABOUT IT LIKE THAT.

IT SOUNDS AWFUL, BUT WHEN MY GRANDMA DIED, I DIDN'T REALLY FEEL SAD. SHE LIVED MILES AWAY, AND I NEVER SAW MUCH OF HER.

IT'S DIFFERENT FOR ME. GRANDMA LIVED WITH US FOR A LONG TIME. WE WERE VERY CLOSE.

Tina is upset because she feels that she did not have the chance to say goodbye.
This can be hard to deal with whether death is sudden or expected. You may be left feeling guilty and sad because of things you did, or did not, say or do before someone's death. It is important to remember that you are not in any way to blame for the person's death.

The way in which people react to the news of a death can vary according to the situation.
When death is unexpected, the shock might be overwhelming at first. When someone has been ill for a long time, those close to him or her may have had time to adjust and prepare themselves for the news.

Sometimes people can feel a sense of relief, especially if the person was suffering or in a great deal of pain. This can be a difficult emotion to accept. There is no right or wrong way to react. However you react to the news, it does not mean that your grief is any less real or sincere than someone else's.

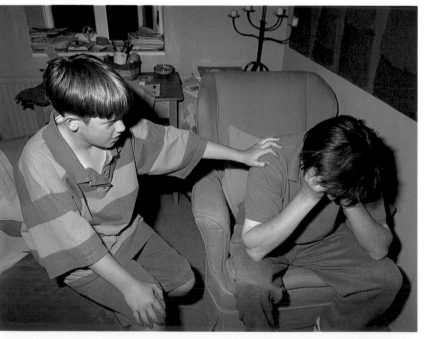

Many people cry when someone they were close to has died.
But not everyone cries, and this does not mean that their emotions for the person are any less strong. Some will cry more than others, and at different times. Crying is sometimes wrongly thought of as a sign of weakness. You may have heard it said that boys and men should not cry. This is not true. It's okay to cry and it's okay not to cry. People express their feelings in very different ways.

FUNERALS AND RITUALS

IT IS IMPORTANT FOR MANY PEOPLE TO PAY THEIR LAST RESPECTS AND TO SAY GOODBYE TO THE PERSON WHO HAS DIED.

A funeral is an official ceremony at which people can do this. It usually involves burial of the body or "cremation," when the body is burned. In most countries, before a funeral is able to take place, a death certificate will be issued, stating the cause of death. This will have been determined by an official such as the person's doctor or an authorized medical examiner, who may sometimes need to do tests to find out the exact cause. The nature of a funeral or ritual to mark the death of someone can depend on several factors, such as the person's country, culture, and religion. It may involve a religious ceremony, or a person's friends talking about what they loved about him or her. Although a funeral is often a sad occasion, it can have a positive side. For many, it is a chance to honor and to say goodbye to someone they cared about. It is also a time when friends and family can offer each other support and understanding.

In some cultures, wearing black is considered a sign of respect for the dead person. In others, it is traditional for relatives to dress in white.

▽ The funeral was due to take place a few days later.

ANNIE'S TOO YOUNG TO UNDERSTAND WHAT'S HAPPENING. IT WOULD BE TOO UPSETTING FOR HER. SHE'S GOING TO MRS. WHITE'S FOR THE AFTERNOON.

ARE YOU SURE YOU BOTH WANT TO GO? I WON'T BE UPSET IF YOU DECIDE YOU'D RATHER STAY HERE.

NO. WE WANT TO GO.

▽ At the service, the family cried a lot. Afterward, Tina tried to comfort her mom.

COME ON, MOM. DON'T CRY. I CAN'T BEAR TO SEE YOU SO UPSET.

MOM'LL BE ALRIGHT, TINA. SHE NEEDS TO CRY NOW. DON'T WORRY.

IT WAS LIKE SAYING GOODBYE AGAIN, WASN'T IT?

THAT'S PART OF WHA A FUNERAL'S ALL ABOU IT GIVES PEOPLE A CHANCE TO REMEMBER SOMEONE AND THINK ABOUT THEM.

▽ The next day at school, his friends asked Mark about the funeral.

I'VE NEVER BEEN TO ONE. I DON'T THINK I EVER WANT TO GO.

IT WASN'T SO BAD, THOUGH EVERYONE CRIED A LOT. GRANDMA WAS BURIED NEXT TO GRANDPA.

I DON'T WANT TO BE BURIED WHEN I DIE. I WANT TO BE CREMATED, LIKE MY UNCLE WAS.

HE HAS A GOLD PLAQUE IN A PLACE CALLED A GARDEN OF REMEMBRANCE. I THINK THAT WOULD BE NICER THAN BEING IN THE GRAVEYARD, WITH ALL THOSE WEIRD STONES AND THINGS.

THE ANCIENT EGYPTIANS USED TO BE BURIED WITH ALL KINDS OF TREASURES. THEY WERE FOR IN THE NEXT WORLD. I LIKE THAT IDEA.

WHAT ABOUT REINCARNATION? SOME PEOPLE BELIEVE YOU COME BACK AS SOMEONE OR SOMETHING ELSE AFTER DEATH. I DON'T THINK IT'S TRUE, DO YOU?

IN MY RELIGION, EVERYONE WHO DIES IS CREMATED. WE DON'T BURY PEOPLE.

WHO KNOWS? ARE WE GOING TO PLAY FOOTBALL? ARE YOU COMING TO THE PARK AFTER SCHOOL, MARK?

△ The friends began to talk about different beliefs.

◁ Mark said no. He was meeting Julian Idika. The two of them had become good friends.

Annie's parents think it's best that she doesn't go to the funeral. Younger children may not always fully understand the significance of funerals. Some might be confused or even frightened by what happens. Although adults often believe they are protecting them by not allowing them to attend, some young people might be upset at being excluded. They may want the same chance as everyone else to say goodbye. Each situation needs to be judged individually.

Tina hates to see her mom upset. But her dad realizes that she needs to express her grief. A funeral is a time when most people will experience intense emotions. It is never easy to see those you love suffering, and your immediate reaction might be to want to help stop their pain. But this is not always possible. Funerals can bring out feelings that people have been bottling up because they are so difficult to face. Telling someone not to cry will not help them to deal with those feelings.

People symbolize death in different ways. This depends on religious and cultural beliefs, and such things as family traditions. Some cultures have annual celebrations or ceremonies at which the spirits of the dead are honored with gifts. These may be very happy occasions. Many people commemorate the deceased with a plaque or headstone.

GRIEF

COMING TO TERMS WITH THE FACT THAT SOMEONE CLOSE HAS DIED CAN TAKE A LONG TIME.

Many people will experience grief after a bereavement. This is often a mixture of strong physical and emotional reactions. It may also be called mourning.

The responses can be similar to those of someone who has been told that he or she is dying. People may be unable to believe what has happened, or they may become depressed and angry. Others feel that their own life is no longer worth

living. They might have difficulty sleeping or have headaches. Most people experience many different feelings at the same time. Someone may appear to be coping, then might suddenly break down in tears. They may cry a lot or show no interest in what is going on around them. It can seem as if there are no limits to how terrible you are feeling, or as though the grief will never end. Very young children might not be able to put their emotions into words; instead, they may act them out. It is very important for everybody to have the chance to grieve.

When some people are grieving, they may seem to lose their temper more quickly than usual. This is often because they are trying to cope with so many confusing emotions.

24

▽ One weekend, Mark and Tina met Julian and his mom in town. Mrs. Idika asked how they were both feeling.

WE'RE OK. IT'S MOM I'M WORRIED ABOUT. SHE'S TAKEN GRANDMA'S DEATH REALLY BADLY.

IT'S BEEN TWO MONTHS NOW SINCE SHE DIED. I THOUGHT MOM WOULD FEEL BETTER BY NOW.

IT'S NOT THAT SIMPLE, MARK. IT CAN TAKE A LONG TIME TO GET OVER A DEATH. IT'S MORE THAN A YEAR SINCE FRANKIE DIED, AND I STILL CRY ABOUT HIM SOMETIMES.

BUT FRANKIE WAS VERY YOUNG AND HE DIED IN AN ACCIDENT. GRANDMA WAS QUITE OLD, AND WE KNEW SHE WAS GOING TO DIE.

THAT DOESN'T NECESSARILY MAKE IT EASIER WHEN IT HAPPENS. LOSING A CHILD IS TERRIBLE, BUT ANYONE'S DEATH, NO MATTER HOW OLD THEY ARE OR HOW THEY DIED, CAN BE AS DIFFICULT TO COPE WITH.

▽ The following weekend, Tina and Mark invited some friends over. Julian arrived first.

△ Mrs. Idika said that it was not always possible to know how grief would affect people.

GOOD TO FINALLY MEET YOU, JULIAN.

WHAT ARE YOU UP TO, ANNIE? ARE YOU KNITTING?

THOSE ARE GRANDMA'S NEEDLES. SHE USED TO LOVE TO KNIT. I'LL TEACH YOU TO KNIT PROPERLY IF YOU LIKE, ANNIE.

I DON'T WANT TO TALK ABOUT GRANDMA. I DON'T LIKE GRANDMA. SHE DIDN'T LOVE ME OR SHE WOULDN'T HAVE GONE AWAY.

▽ Mark apologized to Julian and they all went out into the garden.

△ Annie threw down the needles and ran out of the room.

SORRY ABOUT THAT.

THAT'S OK. I KNOW HOW ANNIE'S FEELING. WHEN FRANKIE DIED, I USED TO HATE HIM FOR LEAVING ME BEHIND. MOM MISSED FRANKIE SO MUCH—FOR A WHILE IT WAS LIKE I DIDN'T EXIST.

IT TOOK MOM A LONG TIME TO COME TO TERMS WITH HIS DEATH. THINGS ARE BETTER NOW, AND WE TALKED ABOUT IT A LOT. BUT I STILL GET ANGRY SOMETIMES.

IT'S ONLY NATURAL. I STILL GET UPSET ABOUT GRANDMA. LOOK, HERE ARE THE OTHERS.

△ They went over to join their friends.

As Mark knows, the death of a baby or child can be particularly difficult to come to terms with. The death of someone at a young age may seem unfair, because the person has been cheated of the chance to grow up. Parents and brothers and sisters may be devastated by the loss and find it difficult to accept. It can be very hard for the other children in the family if their parents are so distressed that they seem to be ignoring them. But the grief their parents are experiencing may temporarily seem to block out everything else. Parents may be feeling guilty about their child's death, believing that, as parents, they should have been capable of doing something to prevent it, even when there was nothing they could have done.

Mrs. Idika knows that there is no set time at which grief begins or ends. How you cope with your grief will depend on your own personality, the circumstances of the death, and the support you receive from others.

Julian has said that he hated his brother after he died, because of the effect that his death had on his mom. Death forces changes in people's lives. It is normal for people to experience feelings of anger toward the dead person. They may blame him or her for leaving. They may feel let down because the death has created the situation in which they now find themselves. It is not unusual for people who are very upset to say and do things that they may not really mean or might later regret.

LEARNING TO COPE

GIVEN TIME, MOST PEOPLE COME TO TERMS WITH EVEN THE MOST DIFFICULT OF FEELINGS.

Going on with your own life does not mean that you have to forget about the person who has died, or that you are betraying him or her in any way.

We cannot stop our own lives because of the death of someone else. Nor is it likely that the deceased would want us to. It can be useful to talk about how you feel, and perhaps to discuss the dead person with others who knew him or her. Some have found that keeping busy helps them to cope with their grief. There is nothing wrong with this, as long as they do not simply bottle up their emotions or try to avoid having to face them. As people's feelings of grief become easier to bear, they may sometimes feel guilty about lighter moments, making new friends, or having a good time. But there is no reason why anyone should feel that it is wrong to enjoy life. Mourning does not have to consist of only unhappy moments, even though at first it can seem as though the sadness might never go away.

You may feel sad at different times – for example when a particular place or thing reminds you of the person. But this is a natural part of the grieving process. It need not stop you from living your life to the fullest.

▽ A few weeks later, Tina found Mark in his room, writing a letter.

IT'S A LETTER TO GRANDMA. IT WOULD HAVE BEEN HER BIRTHDAY TOMORROW.

I KNOW. WHY WRITE A LETTER, THOUGH? IT'S NOT AS THOUGH SHE CAN ACTUALLY READ IT.

THAT'S NOT THE POINT. I STILL WANTED TO TELL HER HOW I FELT. ANYWAY, YOU STILL TALK TO HER SOMETIMES. I'VE HEARD YOU.

I SUPPOSE I DO. IT JUST HELPS TO TALK ABOUT THINGS, THE WAY WE USED TO WHEN SHE WAS ALIVE. I TRY TO IMAGINE WHAT GRANDMA WOULD SAY.

△ Mark finished his letter. He went to show it to his mom.

IT'S LOVELY, DARLING. WHAT A NICE THING TO DO.

I DID IT BECAUSE I WAS AFRAID OF FORGETTING ABOUT GRANDMA. SOMETIMES, WHEN I AM HAVING A GOOD TIME, I FEEL GUILTY ABOUT IT.

I WAS VERY UPSET AT FIRST. I DON'T KNOW WHERE I'D HAVE BEEN WITHOUT YOU TWO AND YOUR DAD. BUT FEELINGS DO CHANGE GRADUALLY. IT'S OK TO FEEL HAPPY. YOUR GRANDMA WOULDN'T HAVE WANTED YOU TO BE SAD ALL THE TIME.

△ Mrs. Burton said that neither of them should feel guilty about enjoying themselves. They'd never forget Grandma.

△ Mrs. Burton suggested they arrange to go out for a day the following weekend.

▷ Mark and Tina invited Julian and Mrs. Idika and some of their other friends along too. They all went to the park.

YOUR MOM SEEMS A LOT HAPPIER NOW

IT WAS GRANDMA'S BIRTHDAY LAST WEEK AND THAT WAS A BIT DIFFICULT, BUT OTHERWISE THINGS ARE MUCH BETTER NOW.

WE ALL WENT TO GRANDMA'S GRAVE AND TOOK SOME FLOWERS. IT WAS SAD, BUT QUITE NICE TOO.

I KNOW. SPECIAL OCCASIONS ARE ALWAYS HARD. COME ON YOU GUYS. HELP ME GET THESE BOATS IN THE WATER.

Special times, such as birthdays or holidays, may bring back the memory of the dead person.
Sometimes this can also bring with it the same kind of emotions you felt immediately after his or her death. This is natural and will become easier to handle with time. Most people are eventually able to separate the memory of the person from the pain of their grief. Remembering people is important and can give a lot of pleasure. As you begin to get on with your life, you may find your mind is no longer filled with thoughts of the dead person. This is normal. Not thinking about someone all the time does not make that person or their memory any less important to you. It can make your memories even more special.

It is difficult when the person who has died is the one you really want to talk to about the way you are feeling.
Expressing emotions in practical ways, like Mark has done, by writing a letter or poem can help people to work through their grief or to say things they would have wanted the deceased to know. This can help especially if someone did not have the chance to say goodbye.

Mrs. Burton knows that, through this difficult time, it is important to have the help and support of others.
After a person has died, you may think you are not able to talk to the people you would normally turn to, because they are also grieving. But as long as everyone is willing, sharing your grief with others who are feeling the same way can help you all.

WHAT CAN WE DO?

HAVING READ THIS BOOK, YOU WILL UNDERSTAND THAT DEATH AND DYING ARE A NATURAL PART OF ALL OUR LIVES.

You will know how important it is to express grief and to offer and receive the support needed.
There may be times when you feel you do not know the right words to say.
Just being there for people can help, or giving practical assistance, perhaps by cooking, shopping, or looking after pets for people who are grieving. If you yourself are experiencing feelings of grief, you will know that these can be very difficult to handle, but that this should become easier with time. There is no need to feel that you cannot express your emotions.

Allied Youth and Family Counseling Center
310 N. Windomere
Dallas, TX 75208
214-943-1044

Kids' Fund
P.O. Box 829
Planetarium Station
New York, NY 10024
212-580-8228

Family Resource Coalition
20 N. Wacker Drive
Suite 1100
Chicago, IL 60606
312-338-0900

ADULTS NEED TO BE AWARE THAT THEY MAY SPARE YOUNG PEOPLE MORE PAIN BY SPEAKING HONESTLY AND SIMPLY TO THEM ABOUT DEATH, RATHER THAN AVOIDING THE SUBJECT OR TELLING HALF-TRUTHS.

Finding the right words can be difficult, especially if you feel uncomfortable about discussing the issues, or are grieving yourself.
Adults and young people who have read this book together may like to talk about their feelings. Anyone who would like more information or would like to speak to someone not directly involved may obtain advice or support from the organizations listed.

Association for Death Education and Counseling
638 Prospect Avenue
Hartford, CT 06105-4298
860-232-4825

The National Board For Certified Counselors
3D Terrace Way
Greensboro, NC 27403
910-547-0607

The Education Development Center
55 Chapel Street
Newton, MA 02158
800-225-4276

Center For Family Support
386 Park Avenue South
New York, NY 10016
212-889-5464

The Dougy Center
3909 SE 52nd Avenue
P.O. Box 86852
Portland, OR 97268
503-775-5683

The National Association of Social Workers
750 First Street NE
Suite 700
Washington, DC 20002
202-408-8600

National Hospice Organization
1901 North Moore Street
Suite 901
Arlington, VA 22209
704-243-5900

Help Inc.
638 South Street
Philadelphia, PA 19147
215-924-4096

Compassionate Friends
P.O. Box 3696
Oak Brook, IL 60522-3696
630-990-0010

INDEX

Photocredits
All the pictures in this book are by Roger Vlitos apart from pages: 4, 11 top,12: Eye Ubiquitous; 14 top: Spectrum; 14 bottom, 15, 17 bottom, 23 bottom: Frank Spooner. The publishers wish to acknowledge that all of the photographs in this book have been posed by models.